GREEN BAY PACKERS

Green, Gold, and Proud

PORTRAITS, STORIES, AND TRADITIONS
OF THE GREATEST FANS IN THE WORLD

Photography	**Curt Knoke**
Foreword	**Bob Harlan**
Reflections	**Bart Starr**
Essays	**Bill VanLannen**

TRIUMPH
BOOKS
CHICAGO

Foreword

There are so many words to describe Green Bay Packers fans: *loyal, knowledgeable, passionate, forgiving.*

How else do you explain that every game at Lambeau Field since 1960 has been sold out, that there are still 68,000 names on the waiting list for tickets, and that Packers fans put the names of their newborn babies on the waiting list, hoping the youngster will be able to obtain seats in the historic stadium by the time they are 35 or 40?

But most important of all, the fans actually own the Packers. In the 86-year history of the franchise, approximately 110,000 fans have purchased stock in four separate drives. In the most recent drive, in 1998, the Packers added 106,000 new owners including individuals from all 50 states, Guam, and the U.S. Virgin Islands.

When the Packers won Super Bowl XXXI in 1997, National Football League commissioner Paul Tagliabue said the victory was the best thing to happen to pro sports in years because the Packers are "blue-collar America, small-town America, and, most importantly, they are owned by the fans."

We agree. Our fans—our owners—are truly the best in all of sports, and they make Green Bay the most enthusiastic football town in the country. We are fortunate to have them, and we deeply appreciate them.

—Bob Harlan

Reflections

I will never forget the first time we returned from a championship game on the road while playing for the Green Bay Packers. We had lost a close, hard fought game to the Philadelphia Eagles, the only loss we ever experienced in ten playoff games under Coach Lombardi. As we landed in Green Bay, we were amazed to see waves of fans waiting for us at the airport. We knew our fans were special, but at that moment we discovered that their sense of loyalty and passion was unsurpassed in the NFL.

During the rest of my career and afterward, I was blessed to meet thousands of wonderful individuals who comprise the Packers Nation. Most of these people, of course, happen to live in Wisconsin, but it is amazing how often we meet Packers fans in every state of our union. Each of them speaks of the Packers with admiration and devotion. There truly is nothing like it anywhere, and it flows from the fact that Green Bay is the smallest major sports town in the country. Nowhere else does the success of a team mean as much to a community as it does in Green Bay, Wisconsin.

I have not lived in Green Bay for almost two decades, but my feelings for the Packers fans grow stronger every year.

—Bart Starr

fan

Function: noun
Etymology: probably short for fanatic

1 an enthusiastic devotee (as of a sport or a performing art) usually as a spectator

2 an ardent admirer or enthusiast (as of a celebrity or a pursuit)

Christie, Nathan, and Carter Kelley
(with nurse, Holly Neuman)

St. Mary's Hospital
Green Bay, Wisconsin

For as long as I can remember, I've been a Packers fan. It's a way of life, living in Green Bay. But, with the birth of my son, Carter, everything seems to have taken on new meaning. The relationship between this community and the Green Bay Packers is more significant than that of any other team—anywhere. It's a relationship that offers many meaningful lessons. We learn about commitment, respect, hard work, team spirit, and perseverance. We learn that it's OK to dream. And, if things don't work out quite as planned, we learn to appreciate accomplishments and turn our attention to the future.

That might sound a bit weighty. But, one day after God blessed us with our son's birth, these are the thoughts running through my mind. We've signed Carter up for season tickets. Being 68,265th in line, however, I plan on teaching him what it means to be a Packers fan long before we're sharing seats at Lambeau field.

MY FIRST PACKERS GAME

above (left to right) Alex and Barry Fife, Green Bay, WI I Emy and Cathi Burish, Manitowoc, WI I Amy and Teegan Vangheem, Green Bay, WI
opposite (left to right) George-Anna and Pat Marquart, Rhinelander, WI I Janet and Melissa Sargent, Cedarburg, WI I Courtney and Curt Peronto, Green Bay, WI I Johnathan and Paul Bohnen, St. Germain, WI

Mike Seavert
New Berlin, Wisconsin

Being a Packers fan is like being part of an extended family. You get to experience the games, practices, and events with other dedicated fans. There are going to be times of surprises, frustration, and milestones, like the Packers-Raiders game I attended in December 2003. A remarkable game! I wish I could see Brett Favre perform that well again in person.

Besides having a love for the Green and Gold, one reason I joined the Packers Partners fan club is the group of people who belong to it. We are dedicated fans, and having others around to share the experience with is well worth it. Speaking of sharing experiences, I like to share them with those close to me. That's where my students and families in the Whitnall School District come in. They are like a family to me.

My classroom is set up like a football field, with two fake goal posts and Packers novelty items covering the room. Worksheets handed out in class are always green, gold, or white in color. Students earn "Packer Backer Dollars" for good grades and class participation, which they can use to purchase raffle tickets twice a year for prizes, including Packers-autographed items. We also throw tailgate parties every time the Packers play a Monday night game. My students are always aware of when there are autograph signings and other Packers events, so they can enjoy the experience as well.

Sean Patrick O'Donoghue
(by Kim O'Donoghue, mother)
Dove Canyon, California

An absolutely incredible dream come true!

It all happened when Make-A-Wish granted our son Sean's wish to meet Brett Favre and the Green Bay Packers. Friday, October 8, 2004, the limo pulled up to our house and whisked us off on a journey that will always be in our hearts. We walked the halls of greats. We went into the locker room where Sean was surprised with his own locker next to Brett Favre's. Then we went to practice with the entire Packers team. Sean was surprised once again when asked to huddle up, call some plays, and then call the practice. Coach Sherman invited us to join them for lunch. Sunday morning we met Brett. He talked with Sean and gave him some tips on how to throw the ball. Brett asked Sean what the team needed to do to improve, to which Sean replied, "Dude, score some touchdowns!" We watched that game as if it were our first. We were in awe of every single moment—all the kindness everyone showed to us as no other organization could. We are one of the Pack!

Thank you to the entire Packers organization; you truly live up to the reputation you have earned! You are an inspiring, blessed organization, and your dedication and spirit have been rewarded with loyal, adoring fans!

"I think it's entirely fitting that the Packers take a leading role in honoring their fans for their longtime loyalty and commitment —particularly when you consider that it's the fans who own this football team. It's an idea that's probably long overdue."

—Bob Harlan

above (clockwise from upper left) Nicole Staudenmaier and Alex Brown, Green Bay, WI | Barbara, Star, Tiffany, and Sky Ferguson, Houston, TX; Robert Crow, Marion, LA | Charlie Bucholtz and Tom, Tony, and Nikki Francois, Sun Prairie, WI | Jarred and Joey Pribek, Kewaunee, WI | Finbar, Patrick, Kim, and Cori O'Donoghue, Dove Canyon, CA

Greg, Jill, Ben, Jesse, and Reily Sieren

Wind Lake, Wisconsin

Growing up in Minnesota, my father was a die-hard Packers fan who always preached to me about the history, tradition, and winning ways of the Packers. He always told me that they have the most loyal fans. Many years later, when I finally had the chance to visit Green Bay and the Packers Hall of Fame, I was moved in a spiritual kind of way. All the things that my father had spoken of about the Packers I now understood and recognized. Being a Packers fan is about winning, history, tradition, and loyalty. It's about family—our Packers' family, our team, our town, the fans. The most important thing to me about being a Packers fan is sharing with my children the rich history and tradition of the Packers. It's about creating another bond with the team and teaching another generation, so Packers history and tradition will continue for years to come.

above (left to right) Stew Jr. and Stewart Mills III, Appleton, WI I Mark and Tony Stella, Eagle, WI; Jacob and Kendall Smith, Mukwonago, WI
opposite (left to right) Loren and Thomas Passehl, Green Bay, WI I Brian, David, and Jon Mansfield, Honeoye Falls, NY I Breck and Todd Reich, and Tony Commodore, Union Grove, WI

Bicycle Built for Two

Packers fans descend upon training camp with the timeliness of a Capistrano swallow to take up roost along the fence lining the Packers' practice field.

Each training camp session is attended by as many as three thousand fans, with some practices drawing far more onlookers, depending upon the team's expected fortunes for the upcoming season. The Packers Country Regional Tourism Office estimates that one hundred thousand of these "railbirds" flock to training camp annually, with an estimated economic impact on the area of $35 million.

No one is exactly sure when it began, but Packers players have been riding local kids' bikes to training camp practices for more than 40 years. According to team officials, the tradition is believed to have originated in 1961, when the Packers constructed a new administration building on the stadium's north concourse.

Vince Lombardi, ever the innovator, was the first coach to ask his players to ride bikes to practice in an effort to deepen the team's unique relationship with its fans. Efforts by the players to select bikes worthy of their stature can prove quite comical. Upon finding something suitable, some players opt to use the same bike time and time again while striking up a relationship with the bike's owner for the duration of training camp. Other players are less selective, trying a number of bikes before settling on something expedient.

The Packers are one of only a few teams to hold formal, daily autograph-signing sessions during training camp. Select fans lining the fence are randomly tapped by representatives of the team to enter the practice field at the conclusion of practice. Then various items, ranging from footballs to ballcaps, can be signed by a host of players seated at a shaded table.

Resourceful autograph seekers who failed to be tapped often do just as well by approaching their favorite players as they make their way from the field to the locker room. The players are encouraged to meet the fans' requests as best they can without losing sight of their primary objective—making the team.

The Packers Experience, located in the Lambeau Field concourse, welcomed 36,563 children during a five-week run held during Training Camp 2004. Kids of all ages flocked to the area before and after training-camp practices to participate in hands-on activities that included an obstacle course, football toss and kick, and other football-related activities.

A stadium tour in the redeveloped Lambeau Field was a hot ticket during Training Camp 2004, with nearly twenty-four thousand patrons taking advantage of the opportunity to walk through the players' tunnel and onto Lambeau Field. To accommodate the strong demand, tours of 20–30 patrons were run every 15 minutes—32 tours each day.

Bart Boyden

Green Bay, Wisconsin

My name is Bart Boyden and, it's true, I'm named after Bart Starr. I was born July 3, 1962, at a time when the Packers were just establishing their dynasty. To be named after a man like Bart Starr is a great honor. I cannot think of a single human being with more class and integrity.

I've attended every home "Green Package" Packers game since 1987. The idea of a Packers Car just kind of happened over time. My dad had a green Pontiac Catalina that slowly evolved into a Green and Gold tailgating machine. When it came time to retire the Pontiac in 1990, I purchased a blue 1972 Cadillac. Over time, it too transformed into a Green and Gold center for tailgating culture. The car provides friends and family with a place to gather—a place to rekindle relationships, share memories, and establish camaraderie.

above (clockwise from upper left) Shawn Postell, Wrightstown, WI; Dan Palmer, Shawano, WI; Ken Petersen, De Pere, WI; John Kolar, Bob Balsley, and Kevin Crocker, Green Bay, WI
opposite (left to right) Carrie Zoromski and Carrie Madson, Wausau, WI I Kim Heinzen, Highbridge, WI I Marta Schee, Lebanon, NJ; Kathi Riley, Cary, IL

"Without the fans there would be no game."

—Nick Barnett

Doug Burris
Shawano, Wisconsin

I have been a dedicated Packers fan since the team played at City Stadium. That's where I saw my first game. In 1957, when Packers stadium first opened for business, I sat on the top row in the south end zone. Whenever the Packers played, I wanted to be there.

When the new stadium was built in 1957, its seats were not sold out. Stan & Bud's, a bistro located on Shawano's Main Street, had been a Packers ticket distributor since the twenties. They bought 350 season tickets. There were a tremendous number of Packers fans in Shawano, so Stan and Bud sold tickets to their patrons and organized bus trips whenever the Packers played in Milwaukee or Green Bay.

Around 1980 I managed to get four season tickets from them—a very happy day, indeed. I sat in Section 105, Row 23, at the north end of the stadium. The sun was hot in the early fall, but offered relief in the cold of winter.

Stan and Bud retired and their bar changed hands a number of times. I purchased it in 1991. My son, Mike, managed the place. As part of the deal, I got 331 of the original 350 season tickets. Today, we still organize bus trips. Daryl and Harriet Dehnke bring a busload full of fans from Eau Claire whenever the Packers play in Green Bay. That's part of the Green Bay Package. There are so many great experiences associated with selling Packers tickets. You meet and talk to so many fine fans. People call in from Kentucky, Florida, California . . . all over the place. When you get on a bus with these fans, you feel their excitement and joy. It's a wonderful experience. They've been a pleasant addition to my life.

opposite John Ventriello, Monroe Township, NJ above (clockwise from left) Diane Woolford, Escanaba, WI |
Allison Hotchkiss (a.k.a. Kitty Lambeau), Green Bay, WI | Greg Bastien and Chad Vanderlogt, Green Bay, WI | Karl Hanson, Eau Claire, WI

35

Gary and Esther Wrobel

La Crosse, Wisconsin

Esther and I have been Packers fans for more than 45 years and have held season tickets since 1977. We were on the waiting list for the Green Package for 28 years—17 years for the Gold Package. We've been collecting Packers souvenirs for all of those 45 years. We are charter members of America's Pack Fan Club and Packers Partners fan club. We love the Pack and always will. Go, Pack!

Tony LeMieux
Green Bay, Wisconsin

Since I was a kid, I've been a Packers fan.

Nearly two decades ago, I traveled around the Midwest investigating sports bars. Then, in 1990, Pat Quinn and I opened what's known as the first true sports bar in Green Bay. We named it "Gippers" after George Gipp, the Notre Dame football legend. The walls are crammed with sports memorabilia—from Reggie White- and Brett Favre-signed jerseys, to a Babe Ruth-signed baseball . . . and, we even have a 1997 Superbowl team-signed cheese head.

At Gippers we offer fun, football-themed food and drinks for the most discerning of Packers fans. Game day here is always an event!

Christopher Handler
Green Bay, Wisconsin

Born in 1956, at nine years old I was hopping over the fence at Lambeau Field, with a boost from another fan, guarding each other from the ushers for a free three quarters of the game. I was very proud to be a Packers fan at that age and it stuck with me all my life. When I was 14 years old I sold hot dogs at the games. Then, four years later, I sold beer. I loved being a fan of the Green Bay Packers.

In 1972 I put my name in for season tickets. Finally, 32 years later, I received a letter from the Packers' ticket office that my number had come up. My wife, Jan, my daughters, Alexandra and Brooke, and I now own four tickets.

I am a local painter and handyman and saw an article in the *Press Gazette* that a real estate agent was looking for a painter to paint the famous Lombardi Avenue fence. I called her up to voluntarily offer my services. She said, "The job is yours." She sold the house, which is located on Shadow Lane. The Lombardi Avenue fence has received a new slogan each year for the past 21 years. I feel great to be part of history with every stroke of paint I put on the fence. GO, PACK, GO!

Supper Time

Packers fans view pre-game preparations as an opportunity to check equipment, stock up on supplies, enjoy a brat or hotdog, and get into uniform. They can be as disciplined in their approaches to game day as their favorite players.

Fans have been tailgating prior to Packers games for nearly as long as the team has been in existence. The practice of congregating before kickoff may have been introduced as early as 1923, when the team played at Bellevue Park, a minor league baseball park. By the time City Stadium's spacious parking lots opened in 1957, tailgating had already evolved into an art form.

A half century later, only the very game itself exceeds the pageantry, the color, and the enthusiasm of tailgating. The Lambeau Field parking lot opens four hours prior to kickoff, and tailgaters use that time to construct a makeshift city composed of campers, buses, recreational vehicles, and SUVs. Many of the vehicles come painted in green and gold and bear state-issued Packers license plates or, in some cases, personalized license plates with such inscriptions as "Shareholder," "Starr 15," or "Lambeau." There are vehicles representing nearly all the states.

The Lambeau Field parking lot can host as many as 4,800 cars and yet a friendly, small-town atmosphere pervades the grounds.

Many fans mark their locations with banners or flags that represent their respective hometowns, but strangers are always welcome—even fans of the visiting team! In modest tents one finds the latest in modern accoutrements, including satellite dishes, big screen TVs, and sophisticated stereo systems. Pre-game talk shows and the radio voices of the Green Bay Packers fill the airwaves.

As if they were players donning the uniform, many fans boast their love of their team on their sleeves, their heads, their ears, and just about anywhere else a Packers logo can be prominently displayed. They have earned such monikers as "Packalope," "Titletown's No. 1 Clown," "Saint Vincent," "Kitty Lambeau," "Helmet Head," and "G-Man." The presence of these unique characters is as much a part of the tailgating experience as the beer, brats, and burgers.

Those looking to fire up the grill have a diversity of culinary delights from which to choose. Old family recipes penned on notecards mix well with the latest concoctions downloaded from the Internet. One of the more popular resources is the *Tailgaten Cookbook*, which is updated yearly by the publishers of the *Packer Report*, a weekly newspaper about the team. It contains photos of tailgating fans and more than 150 recipes for everything from meat and seafood to pasta and dessert.

Anne Auchter Olsen
Milwaukee, Wisconsin

I have been a Packers fan for more than 80 years. Now I'm 102, and don't miss a game or news report about my Packers. In 2003 I was a finalist for the Packers Fan of the Year award.

With six brothers in the house, I wouldn't dare not be a fan! We all gathered in the living room and listened attentively to games on the radio. My sister and I owned a car; our brothers did not. We struck a deal: if the boys wanted a ride to the football game, they had to take us along.

In the late forties, we saw our first football game on TV. It was amazing! I attended my first Packers vs. Bears game with my siblings in 1944 at City Stadium, the year the Pack won their sixth NFL title. At 91 years old, I cheered for the Pack in person at one of the last games to be played in Milwaukee.

I look forward to another season with my favorite, Brett Favre, as quarterback. I'd like to leave him with a piece of advice: Brett, throw the ball away. You're no spring chicken anymore! You can't always throw into traffic and reach your receivers.

"Packers fans are honest. They trust us. And, they're always behind the team—win or lose."

—Donald Driver

Dr. Frank "Hank" Urban
Brookfield, Wisconsin

To be a fan of the greatest team in professional sports—the Green Bay Packers—means many things. Among the words that come to mind are *dedication*, *commitment*, *loyalty*, *pride*, *devotion*, and *sacrifice*.

As a lifelong fan of 75 years and having grown up in Green Bay, I have green blood in my veins—all the better to endure the harsh weather conditions when watching the Green and Gold play on the "frozen tundra" at Lambeau Field or when flying to distant playing fields across our great country.

Included in the property of a Packers fan are personalized Packers auto license plates; a Packers shrine; numerous Packers outfits for rain, snow, or heat; a flag for the house and car; and my favorite game day outfit, a Packers hard hat and green and gold saddle shoes.

Ah, the games! One must stay true in the lean times—25 quarterbacks between Bart Starr and Brett Favre—and relish the good times—the Ice Bowl and Super Bowls II, XXXI, and XXXII.

And at home one must continue the legacy. I raised six sons and one daughter. They are die-hard Packers fans who return every year for one game—"Buddy Fest"—a time to celebrate, with face paint, outfits, videos, and wholesome fun, the joy of being a Packers family.

Sister Isaac Jogues Rousseau
Milwaukee, Wisconsin

Green Bay, Wisconsin, 1921. Two beginnings: birth of Marjorie Rousseau and entrance of the Packers into the National Football League. From the beginning I felt there was a destined interchange between us. As a child I knew two football teams, the Green Bay Packers and the Chicago Bears, and learned to growl at the very sound of the rival's name.

Upon entering the convent, I became Sister Isaac Jogues. Wherever I taught—Milwaukee, Chicago, St. Louis, Washington, D.C.—my devotion never wavered. "On you Green and Gold to glory," I would sing above the tumult.

In 2003 I became the sixth honoree to be inducted into the Packers Fan Hall of Fame. Go, Pack, go! Sister I.J. is always with you.

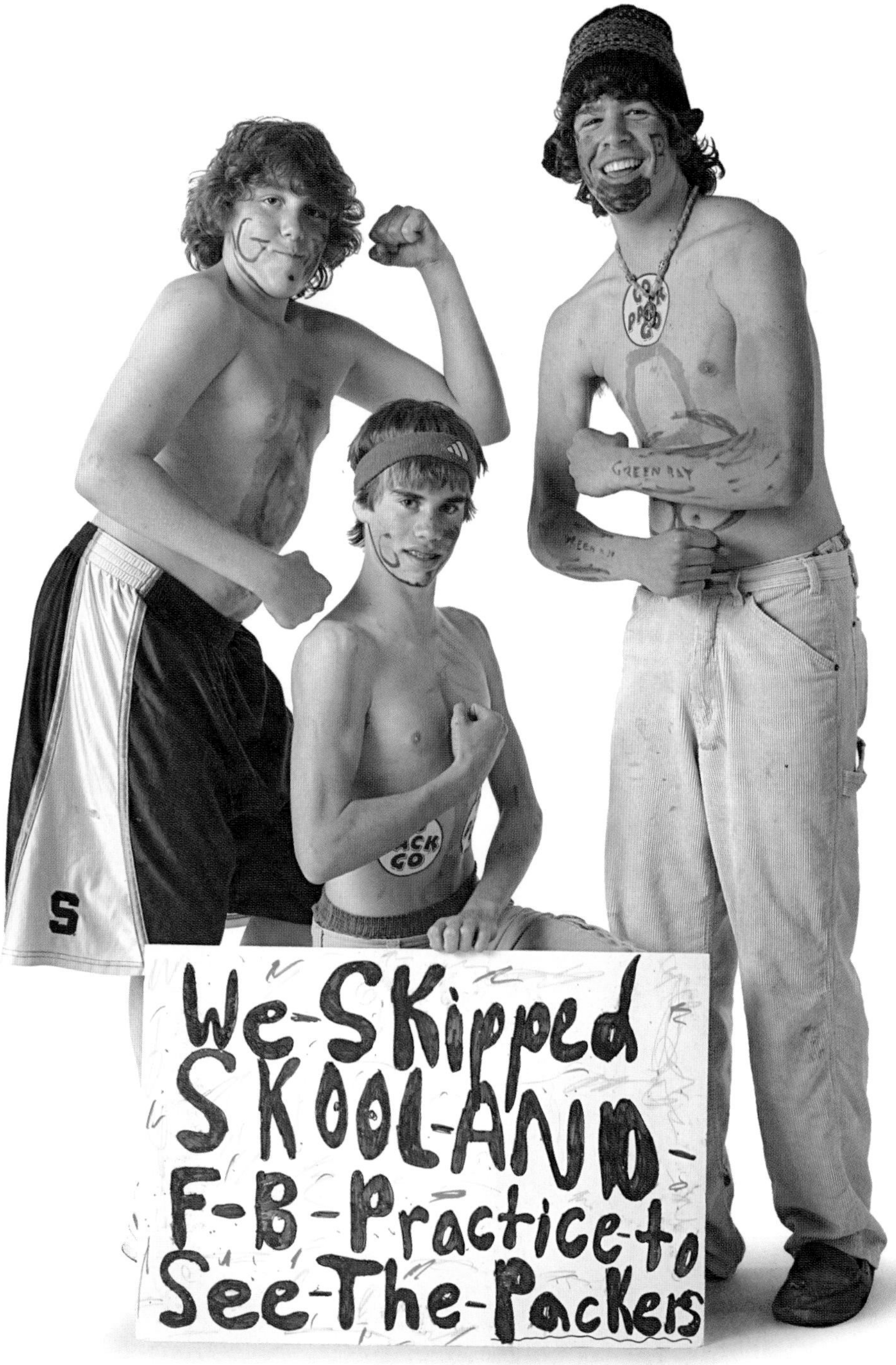
We-SKipped
SKOOL-AND-
F-B-Practice-to
See-The-Packers

Wanda Boggs
Brookfield, Wisconsin

Sundays are for chips, a faithful couch, and the best franchise a fan could ask for. Wisconsin may be known for freezing temperatures, but it's home to the hottest team in football. Win or lose, being a Packers fan is about dignity, integrity, and the relationship between a team and its community. I believe a team should play in the elements, work harder than every blue- and white-collar worker in the state, and they should be owned by people instead of corporations. Welcome to the perfect fan/football partnership. The Green Bay Packers organization recognizes the importance of a dedicated fan base. What other franchise names a fan of the year and honors that individual at their Hall of Fame ceremony? I'm a fan of the Green and Gold because they play to win and they play for me. Like my phone message states: go, Pack, go!

above (clockwise from upper left) David Fisher, Chicago, IL; Jim Rodger and John Pashouwer, Minneapolis, MN | Bill Vargo and Mike Linc, Detroit, MI | Nichole and Ashley Everard, Menominee, MI

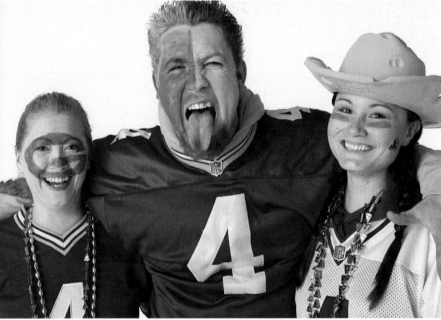

above (clockwise from upper left) Dave (Bully) Bullerman, Savage, MN; Becky Fazer, Milwaukee, WI; Jon Fezatte, Prior Lake, MN I
Sonya Torres-Lemke and JC Fenzl, Oshkosh, WI I Heather and Andrew Smith, and Misty DuPré, Temecula, CA

69

Brad and Kathy Kaufman (with Benji)
Greendale, Wisconsin

Hard work, faithfulness, and honesty are all characteristics that, to me, describe what it takes to be a Packers fan. As a Wisconsin native, it's easy to grow up being a Green Bay Packers fan, but when you realize just how many Packers fans there are worldwide, you get a much deeper respect for the organization. We have met so many terrific people from all over the U.S. and overseas through the official Packers fan club, Packers Partners Club of Champions. We look forward to each game, either tailgating or watching with friends.

I enjoy collecting whatever memorabilia I can get my hands on, including autographs from players. I only collect for myself and would never dream of selling. Autographs are an honor to receive, and they hold memories of meeting the players. Most recently, I got a Packers tattoo for my birthday.

Jim, Scott, Vicki, and Jim Brown
Camp Douglas, Wisconsin

I remember back in the fifties watching Packers games on a black-and-white TV. Reception was such that I thought it was always snowing in Green Bay.

I've always been a Packers fan, and in the nineties I began collecting. It all started with die-cast cars and trucks. Then, in 1996, Simplicity came out with a Packers lawn mower . . . things really got out of hand after that. Seems like if it was green and gold, we bought it. The stock sale was best of all. It was a great feeling to become a shareholder of the Green Bay Packers. I don't think there is a better organization to be involved in.

Our motor home, decked out in Packers colors, makes for very interesting traveling. Driving through Minnesota you'll get a few "thumbs-down" from passers-by, but then they smile and wave. Life is great, but it's just better when you're a Packers Fan.

opposite (left to right) Diane Hogrefe, Lathrop, CA; Jessica Trinkle, Tracy, CA above (left to right) Ron Hoelzel, Darboy, WI |
Lisa and Eric Meglitsch, and Trisha Andrejan, Toledo, OH | Anita Everard and Amy Simonar, Green Bay, WI

Gimme a Pigfoot
(and a Bottle of Beer)

Wherever two or three football fans gather in the name of the Packers, be it a den, neighborhood bar, or stadium restaurant, a festive atmosphere quickly develops.

On game day hundreds of bars and restaurants throughout Wisconsin greet fans with cheese and sausage trays, Johnsonville brats and German potatoes, prizes for the winners of halftime raffles, drink specials, fight songs, and traditional polka music.

Nationwide, Packers fans gather in locations as far afield as Alaska, California, Hawaii, and New York. In Texas, fans flock to Nick's Sports Bar and Grill in Houston, the home of the Cheddarhead Pack of Houston, a club of some 400 members. In Washington, the Northwest Packers Backers meet for Packers games at the Mustard Seed Grill and Pub in Newport Hills. Groups such as these use the Internet as a source of information on where to gather. All seek to create the ambiance of Lambeau Field at a location that can be thousands of miles away from the actual field.

Since the completion of the stadium renovation project, Curly's Pub has become ground zero for Packers fans in Green Bay. "It's really become the heart of the Atrium," says Scott Kleckner, director of operations.

The pub and restaurant hosts an average of three thousand guests the day before home games and as many as ten thousand during home game weekends, according to Kleckner. It's also the site of rowdy postgame radio broadcasts made in front of a live audience.

In recent years the Packers have utilized the additional space provided by the stadium renovation project to host new events at Lambeau Field. Thousands of fans have been drawn to draft day parties, the first ever Fan Fest, and the annual picnic of the Packers Partners fan club. The in-house fan club, which features a message board, boasts more than four thousand members throughout the world.

previous The Brew House, Red River, WI above Packy's Pub, Milwaukee, WI
opposite (top to bottom) Brett's Farmhouse, Milwaukee, WI I Key Deer Bar & Grill, Big Pine Key, FL I Stadium View Sports Bar & Grill, Green Bay, WI

above (top to bottom) "Let's Talk Sports," Tanners Grill and Bar, Kimberly, WI I "Camp Lambeau," Equipment Room, Lambeau Field
opposite Larry McCarren's "Locker Room Live," SC Grand, De Pere, WI

Audrey Misco
Three Lakes, Wisconsin

As far as I know, I am the only person from the North Woods to have been nominated for the Packers Fan Hall of Fame. Though I didn't win, I was thrilled and honored. I've been a Packers fan all my life. My customers at the American Legion Club in Three Lakes, where I tend bar, will vouch for me. Even at 74, I can cheer and yell with the best of them.

My husband, Glenn "Tex" Misco, was also a great Packers fan. He was usher number 53 at the stadium during the Lombardi years, including the Ice Bowl. He passed away September 9, 2001.

I have many Packers memories, but this was the greatest: while enjoying lunch at a supper club in the Green Bay area, I recognized Tony Canadeo seated at the bar. Now 83 years old, he was a running back for the Packers during the forties and early fifties. I just so happened to have his picture, and got him to autograph it for me.

above (left to right) Juan Garcia and Angel Zarenana, Butler, WI opposite (left to right) Dylan Wendt and Luke Merwin, Fond du Lac, WI

Dorothy Hanke
(with daughter Suzi Schoeneich; granddaughters, Tami Roman, Traci Zagrodnik, and Wendi Gerharz; and great granddaughter, Amanda Schoeneich)

Milwaukee, Wisconsin

A true Packers fan is not a fanatic. At times we may be overly enthusiastic and expect to win every game, but we can accept the painful reality of a loss, however undeserved in our eyes. We may be voluble at times, but we do not place blame elsewhere if the team goofed. As my mom used to say, "This too shall pass, and the hurt doesn't hurt so much. Hopefully, they will do better next game, and the skies will be bluer and the sun shine brighter in our hearts."

As long as I can remember I've been a Packers fan and consider them my "alter" family. Even before the Vince Lombardi era, the names Tony Canadeo, Eddie Jankowski, Clarke Hinkle, Don Hutson, and others were familiar to me. With the advent of TV in the forties it was easier to keep track of my team. All the while, my faith never wavered. My selection as the 2004 Packers Fan Hall of Fame Honoree is the best 85th birthday present I could ever receive. Go, Pack, go!

above (left to right) Dakota Legge and Lynn Michko, Palos Park, IL | Chris Reichert, Anacortes, WA | Gary Schmidt, Richfield, WI; Stan Franke, Wauwatosa, WI | Sue, Brian, and Kyle Kenke, New London, WI | Doug McHone, Baraboo, WI

above (left to right) Gary and Bonnie Paul, Green Bay, WI; Dawn and Dale Sisel, Green Bay, WI | Jan and Jim Larson, Appleton, WI | Kathi Kitzke, LaCrosse, WI | Jarreth Haltaufder-Heid and Jean Gollyhon, Green Bay, WI

"The fans expect a lot of us.
That's what I like about Green Bay."

—Kabeer Gbaja-Biamila

opposite Rich Lund, Rapids City, SD **above (clockwise from upper left)** Mike Nolan and Joe Jungwirth, Oshkosh, WI |
Kevin Sweeney, Lakeville, MN | Cindy Dovnik and Lori Olson, Green Bay, WI | Joe Navarro, Madison, WI

93

"The Packers have lots of owners nobody know

— Jim McMahon

nstead of one owner who doesn't know anything."

above (left to right) Jodi and Eric Tarasewicz, Cottage Grove, MN; Katie Mertz, Deer Park, WI I Edith Schneider and Terre Myers, Kaukauna, WI I Dena Kramer, Union Grove, WI; Kim Ketterhagen, Waterford, WI I Jeanne Kemp, Sun Prairie, WI; Vicky Bomkamp, Muscoda, WI opposite (left to right) Amanda Becker and Ryan Dreifke, Kenosha, WI

Edwin Jablonski
Wausau, Wisconsin

How does it feel to be the third Honorary Fan for the Packers Fan Hall of Fame? First and foremost, it has been my greatest honor. Few people have had this privilege. Being honored on the video-boards in front of 68,000 fans is just unbelievable.

Some of my memorable experiences include appearances on TV, radio interviews, and providing information for newspaper articles. Being invited to the Hall of Fame in Canton is still another unforgettable experience. My plaque is displayed both in the Green Bay Hall of Fame as well as in Canton. What an honor!

Five years have passed and I still get phone calls from other fans in recognition. Lots of people from outside the state can't understand the spirit and faithfulness of the Green Bay Packers fans. When we shake hands it sends shivers down our spines. Longtime loyalty, commitment, support, sharing, faithfulness, respect, devotion, and passion . . . that describes the essence of the Green Bay Packers spirit. I know that most Packers fans share these traits.

Mike and Kay Joho
Joliet, Illinois

Mike and I have known each other for decades. We were both born and raised in Manhattan, Illinois, 40 miles southwest of Chicago. Since the late eighties, we would occasionally bump into each other—both decked out in Packers wear— and exchange hellos. Throughout the nineties we'd often see each other at a local bar that televised Packers games. During halftime on

September 13, 1998, Mike asked me to join him in seeing Brett Favre's cameo appearance in *There's Something About Mary*, and our first date was official. On May 20, 2000, we had a simple, elegant wedding and reception—complete with green and gold decorations. Packers mini-helmets served as place cards, and the likes of 15, 4, and 66 served as table numbers.

Today, Mike and I often refer to our home as "Lambeau South," as the Green Bay Packers theme is the focus of nearly every room. We have shared so many wonderful Packers experiences together and love going through life expanding our Packers memories. With our mantra of faith, family, and Packers football, Mike and I can truly say, "Life is good!"

opposite (left to right) Diane Eakins, Grinnell, IA; Jim Lyman, Lutz, FL; Steve Lyman, Clear Lake, IA
above (left to right) Gwen Dohr and Robin Swiatnicki, Peshtigo, WI I Pat Byrne, Fort Wayne, IN; Dick Byrne, Janesville, WI I Jule Hudson and Everett Boldt, Baldwin, WI

Lions and Panthers and Bears…Oh, My!

Packers fans have a grudging respect for the fans of their foes. It's not unlike the relationship of Green Bay's Vince Lombardi and Chicago's George Halas. They held each other in such high esteem that victory by one over the other was all the more sweet.

Mark Schneider, the owner of Glory Days Sports Pub in La Crosse, Wisconsin, often plays host to two bitter border rivals—the fans of the Packers and those of the Minnesota Vikings. Friends and couples in this college town don't always share an affinity for the same team, but they generally get along without bloodshed.

"Most of the smart ones know they share a passion each for his or her own team, so they understand that. Among those that don't understand, it gets tense," says Schneider.

America's Original Sports Bar in the Mall of America, Bloomington, Minnesota, gets around any potential clashes in the heat of the moment by hosting divergent groups of fans in different rooms that are the size of small auditoriums and have their own big-screen TVs.

Fans of different persuasions share a bathroom at the mall, but any conflict between Packers and Vikings fans generally consists of "good-natured ribbing," says Craig Boyte, the director of marketing and promotions at the mall.

Fans of the Packers and Bears, the Packers' traditional rival, peacefully co-exist at Will's Northwoods Inn in Chicago, the very heart of Bears country. Bears fans occupy the front bar and Packers fans the back bar, though in recent years Packers fans have generally had their run of the place. When playing each other they shout back and forth, all in good fun, says the bar's owner.

Jerry Parins, the Packers' director of security, has heard far more good than bad about fan behavior in the four decades he has patrolled the stadium grounds. He cites the NFC championship game against the Carolina Panthers as a prime example of congenial relations among rival teams. Following the game, despite a tough loss, many Carolina fans commented favorably about how they were treated at Lambeau Field.

In listing Lambeau Field among its top 20 sports venues of the 20th century, *Sports Illustrated* has called Packers fans, "rabid but realistic without being rude."

above (left to right) Jamie Tassotti and Aaron Frey, Oshkosh, WI I Kim and Kevin Schaffner, Houston, OH I Jenny and Chris Bradley, Green Bay, WI
opposite (left to right) Maureen and John Dzikonski, Superior, WI

CHICAGO
REAL WOMEN
FOOTBALL
OF YOU, STAY IN THE KITCHEN
BEARS
PACKERS

Ellen Nuebel
(with husband, John)
Libertyville, Illinois

I have been a Packers fan for as long as I can remember. When I was younger I didn't have a big-screen TV; as a matter of fact, the TV we had was smaller than most computer monitors are today. I came from a large family and we always gathered together to watch the games. If we weren't screaming at the team (as if they could hear us), we were yelling at each other to get out of the way! We didn't have a lot of money, so the closest I ever got to a game was visiting my grandmother in Oconto Falls, Wisconsin. That never dampened my loyalty to the Packers or my desire to see a game at Lambeau Field.

The team is very special to me because they care about the community and the fans, not just the money. I've been to a few games in recent years. It's a thrill that is every bit as big as I dreamed it would be.

above (left to right) Don and Brady Dallman, Eric Langman, and Bill Dallman, Manawa, WI

Alan and Nancy Picha
Hillsboro, Wisconsin

Being from Wisconsin and growing up toward the end of the Glory Years probably have the most to do with my becoming a Green Bay Packers fan. As kids of today impersonate star players like Brett Favre, my era grew up adoring the future Hall of Famers such as Bart Starr and Ray Nitschke.

Becoming a collector of sports cards and memorabilia at an early age has led to what I've been told is an "awesome" collection of Packers items. I still have the very first item I purchased as a grade schooler: the ever-loving bobblehead. As an adult, I've had the good fortune of attending Super Bowls XXXI and XXXII; games both home and away; and have met several of the Packers greats over the years. But best of all, my family has chosen to become Packers fans, too. They will carry on the tradition of celebrating one of the greatest sports franchises in the world—one in which I am a shareholder.

As with many fans, the Green and Gold runs deep within me, offering many fantastic opportunities to celebrate and enjoy the Packers spirit—on and off the field.

"It's an honor to play for Green Bay because they're such great fans. They support us regardless of our success, and we feed off their excitement. I hope to be a member of this team for a long, long time. And I will support these fans until the day I retire."

—William Henderson

Jeff and Pam Hewitt
Appleton, Wisconsin

For my wife, Pam, and me, being a Packers fan is a way of life. I guess the obsession began at an early age when I used to have the players ride my bike to and from practice. Being able to interact with the players at such an early age really set the tone, and my fascination grew from there. Supporting a team that is owned by the city and will never move is very comforting. Also, this being the smallest city to support an NFL team speaks volumes about Packers fans. I'm sure just about everyone in this state supports the Packers; some (like my wife and I) choose to do it a little more openly or crazily. If I could have, I would have painted our home's exterior green and gold.

For now, the colors are limited to my rec room, my son Hunter's room, and my boat, which happens to be green and gold with "Go Packers" printed on both sides. Being Packers fans affects our whole family. Hopefully our children will grow up to be Packers fans—I'm not sure they really have a choice!

Jeff Kahlow
Fond du Lac, Wisconsin

I'm sure it helped that, as a child, my favorite color was green. It probably was the deciding factor in choosing my favorite team—the Packers, that is! What two colors go better together than green and gold? When I was a little tyke, I recall my dad screaming out, "Quieeeeeettttt, the Packers game is on!" My brother, sister, and myself were quiet as mice for three hours.

Creativity was in my mom's blood, and as I grew older my appreciation for art grew greater and greater. So what better way to express my love for the Green and Gold than to carve an oversized piece of polyurethane foam, throw some paint on it, slap it on top of my head, and scream, "Go, Pack, go!"

I tip my hat to Tom Murphy, director of the Packers Hall of Fame, who displayed four of my hat creations in the Packers Hall of Fame. What an honor! Thanks to a little push from my brother, I was also named Wisconsin's Ultimate Packers Fan in a statewide competition in 2003. I am now a father of four, with a wonderful wife who surely holds down the fort. I'm proud to be a Green Bay Packers fan! Hi Dad, we miss you!

"Packers fans are behind their team 110 percent."

—Ahman Green

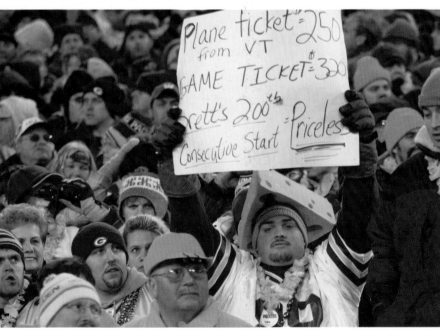

above (left to right) Erica Riedel, Milwaukee, WI I Dan Peggs and Jon Herger, Green Bay, WI I Greg Hiebing, Neenah, WI
opposite (left to right) Josha Khong, Green Bay, WI I Richard W. Hurley, Yonkers, NY

Wendy Smetana
(with funeral director, Dan Malcore)
Green Bay, Wisconsin

I've been a Packers fan for as long as I can remember. I call myself a "die hard" Packers fan, because I have a green and gold casket to prove it. I bought it in 1997 when we won our last Super Bowl. Originally, I'd picked one out in silver and blue, but then I saw an ad for the green and gold model! What choice did I have? I told my boys I want a tailgate party when I die; they laughed, but I'm serious. Every corner of my den is filled with Packers memorabilia. I have a cardboard cutout of Brett Favre in my bedroom, because there's no space anywhere else. What more could you ask for than to see Brett first thing when you wake up?

What I like about being a Packers fan is that Green Bay is a small town that can stand up to the "big boys." I've been a season-ticket holder since 1957. Wherever you go, people ask where you're from. When I say "Green Bay," the response is always "home of the Packers." Then I tell them I've had season tickets for 47 years, and all they can say is "wow!"

above (clockwise from upper left) Jerry Damkot, Sheboygan, WI I Bonnie Johnson, Antioch, IL I Trish Kennedy, New Brighton, MN I Kelly Malucha, West Allis, WI; Brad Helm, Sussex, WI I Johnold Strey Sr., Cedarburg, WI I Katherine Streuber, Las Vegas, NV I Mike Schloemer, Albany, WI I MaryLou Norlander, Milwaukee, WI; Sharon Smith, Rosemont, IL

above (clockwise from left) Steve Keller, Brooklyn, WI | Col. Bill White, Paddock Lake, Salem, WI | Shintaro Araki, Irvington, NY |
Cheryl Wanty, Waupaca, WI; Brenda Hibbard, Appleton, WI; Sharon Roso, Delafield, WI; Sharon VanStiphout, Little Chute, WI

"In Green Bay, more than anywhere else, fans feel like they are part of the team."

—Brett Favre

Packers' Fan
Hall of Fame Inductees

1998	**Mel Knoke, Appleton, WI**
1999	**Louis Gardipee, Black River Falls, WI**
2000	**Ed Jablonski, Wausau, WI**
2001	**Paul Mazzoleni, Green Bay, WI**
2002	**Wanda Boggs, Brookfield, WI**
2003	**Sister Isaac Joques Rousseau, Milwaukee, WI**
2004	**Dorothy Hanke, Milwaukee, WI**

Mel Knoke
(by Curt Knoke, nephew)

Appleton, Wisconsin

Uncle Mel was the consummate Packers fan. He started going to the games back in 1927 in his Model T Ford with his girlfriend and future wife, Leone, and two other guests. They always took guests. During the 63 years they cheered for the Packers, they missed only 13 games; that's just two games per decade! If one couldn't go to the game, the other didn't. At the Hall of Fame induction banquet, Uncle Mel and Aunt Leone were referred to as "the ultimate team for the ultimate team."

He didn't make the banquet. He was hospitalized just two days before. The Packers staged an event in the hospital's banquet room in his honor. There they presented him with the Fan of the Year award, one day before he died.

Uncle Mel and Aunt Leone attended their last game together on a frigid January 12, 1997. It was the championship game that took the Packers to Super Bowl XXXI. That year Uncle Mel gained national attention by way of an NFL commercial that featured him saying, "My name is Mel Knoke, and I feel the power."

Uncle Mel often stated that he had three priorities in life: "the Lord, my wife, and the Green Bay Packers," a team which he never spoke ill of and a team that he took with him to his grave, wearing his trademark Packers wooden bow tie.

I was honored to have inherited two of his season tickets.

Credits

Photographer – Curt Knoke
Creative Director – Kyle Knoke
Art Director – Jeni Moore
Production Artists – Alex Schultz and Timm Buechler
Photo Assistants – Ethan Hoffman, Matt Ludtke,
Bill Rein, Joe Schmidt, and Roger Wilmers
Scouts – Judy Cusick, Donna Gehl,
Tracey Jenks, Gary Knoke, and Kurt Kolosso

Copywriter – Bill VanLannen

Additional photo credits:
Glen Hartjes, Image Studios, Appleton, WI – pg. 90
Tom Krajcik, Bonduel, WI – middle photo, pg. 77

Special thanks to:
Image Studios for their support, encouragement,
and expertise. Appleton Coated, Quebecor World,
and Steen Macek.

And to the following at the Green Bay Packers:
Craig Benzel, Shea Greil, Bob Harlan,
Sarah Koenig, Michelle Palubicki, Aaron Popkey,
Dave Westphal, and Bob Woelfel.

Dustin and Dr. Mike Tucker, Lehigh Acres, FL I Greg Sherwood, Austin, TX I Tracey Nielsen and Courtney Hull, Green Bay, WI I Ryan Day, Beaumont, CA I Troy, Craig, and Jason Peterson, Black River Falls, WI I Lisa Cerkas and Sara